EARLY ROCK

ISBN 0-634-06734-6

HAL•LEONARD®
CORPORATION
7777 W. BLUEMOUND RD. P.O. BOX 13819 MILWAUKEE, WI 53213

Visit Hal Leonard Online at
www.halleonard.com

CONTENTS

ALL SHOOK UP

Words and Music by OTIS BLACKWELL
and ELVIS PRESLEY

AT THE HOP

Words and Music by ARTHUR SINGER,
JOHN MADARA and DAVID WHITE

ALONG COMES MARY

Words and Music by
TANDYN ALMER

BARBARA ANN

Words and Music by
FRED FASSERT

BE-BOP-A-LULA

Words and Music by TEX DAVIS
and GENE VINCENT

19

BLUE SUEDE SHOES

Words and Music by
CARL LEE PERKINS

Brightly, not too fast

Well, it's one for the mon-ey, two for the show,

three to get read-y, now go, cat, go! But don't you

step on my blue suede shoes. You can do an-y-thing _ but lay off of my blue suede shoes. ___

Well, you can knock me down, _ step on my face, _
burn my house, _ steal _ my car, _

slan-der my name all o-ver the place; _
drink _ my ci-der from my old _ fruit jar; _

Do an-y-thing that you

BONY MORONIE

Words and Music by
LARRY WILLIAMS

BO DIDDLEY

Words and Music by
ELLAS McDANIEL

To make his pret - ty ba - by a Sun - day hat. __

Won't you come to my house and rack that bone, __

BOOK OF LOVE

Words and Music by WARREN DAVIS,
GEORGE MALONE and CHARLES PATRICK

BOPPIN' THE BLUES

Words and Music by CARL LEE PERKINS
and HOWARD GRIFFIN

Rhythmic Blues Tempo

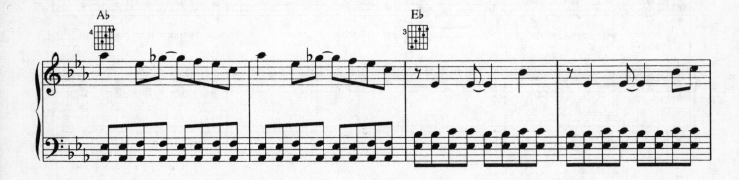

Additional Lyrics

2. We started boppin' but we never stopped,
   It was twelve o'clock when the police knocked,
   I started running for the back door,
   Had the foundations shakin' in that old dance hall,
   I turned around to see the boys in blue,
   And guess what? — They were boppin' the blues.
   To Chorus:

BREAD AND BUTTER

Words and Music by LARRY PARKS
and JAY TURNBOW

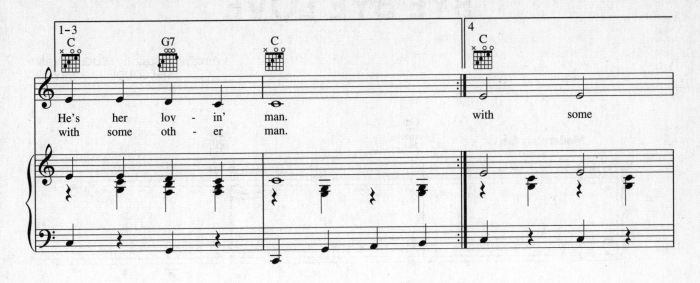

He's   her   lov - in'   man.   with   some
with   some   oth - er   man.

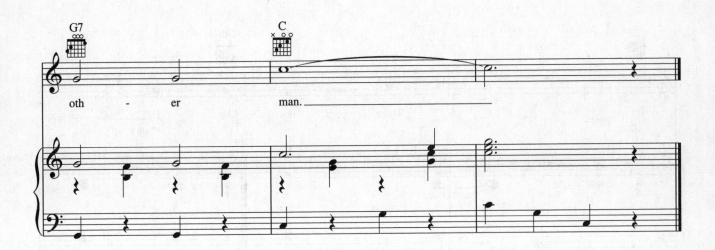

oth - er   man. _____

Additional Lyrics

2. She don't cook mashed potatoes,
   Don't cook T-bone steak.
   Don't feed me peanut butter.
   She knows that I can't take.

3. Got home early one mornin'.
   Much to my surprise
   She was eatin' chicken and dumplin's
   With some other guy.

4. No more bread and butter,
   No more toast and jam.
   I found my baby eatin'
   With some other man.

BYE BYE LOVE

Words and Music by FELICE BRYANT
and BOUDLEAUX BRYANT

There goes my ba - by ____
ro - mance, ____

with some - one new. ____ She sure looks
I'm through with love. ____ I'm through with

CHANTILLY LACE

Moderate Boogie Woogie

Words and Music by
J.P. RICHARDSON

48

CRYING

Words and Music by ROY ORBISON
and JOE MELSON

50

DO WAH DIDDY DIDDY

Words and Music by JEFF BARRY
and ELLIE GREENWICH

DON'T BE CRUEL
(To a Heart That's True)

Words and Music by OTIS BLACKWELL
and ELVIS PRESLEY

Moderately, with half-time feel

You know I can be found.
Ba-by, if I made you mad
Don't stop think-in' of
Instrumental solo

sit-tin' home all a - lone. If
for some-thing I might have said, Come
Don't make me feel this way.

me.

you can't come a-round, at least please tel-e - phone.
please let's for-get the past. The fu-ture looks bright a - head.
on o - ver here and love me. You know what I want you to

DONNA

Words and Music by
RITCHIE VALENS

love _____ my _ girl, _____ Don - na _____ where _____ can you

1 be, _____ where can _ you be?

2 be, _____ where _____ can you be? _____ Oh,

dar - lin' _____ now that you're gone _____ I don't know _____ what I'll __

DREAM LOVER

Words and Music by
BOBBY DARIN

Ev - 'ry night I hope and pray A dream lov - er will come my way, A girl to hold in my arms And know the mag - ic of her charms, Be - cause I

And a hand   that   I   can   hold_____   To feel you near   when

I   grow   old?___ Be-cause I   want _____ a   girl _____ to

call _____   my   own, _____   I want a   dream   lov-er   so

I don't have to dream a-lone._____

EARTH ANGEL

Words and Music by
JESSE BELVIN

Slowly with a beat

DUKE OF EARL

Words and Music by EARL EDWARDS,
EUGENE DIXON and BERNICE WILLIAMS

FUN, FUN, FUN

Words and Music by BRIAN WILSON
and MIKE LOVE

GOOD LOVIN'

Words and Music by RUDY CLARK
and ARTHUR RESNICK

GREAT BALLS OF FIRE

Words and Music by OTIS BLACKWELL
and JACK HAMMER

THE GREAT PRETENDER

Words and Music by
BUCK RAM

Moderately slow

Oh, yes___ I'm the great pre - tend - er, ___ Pre -

tend - in' I'm___ do - in' well; My need is such,___ I pre -

tend too much, I'm lone - ly but no___ one can tell. Oh,

HAPPY, HAPPY BIRTHDAY BABY

Words and Music by MARGO SYLVIA
and GILBERT LOPEZ

A GROOVY KIND OF LOVE

Words and Music by TONI WINE
and CAROLE BAYER SAGER

HANG ON SLOOPY

Words and Music by WES FARRELL
and BERT RUSSELL

HAPPY TOGETHER

Words and Music by GARRY BONNER
and ALAN GORDON

HEARTBREAK HOTEL

Words and Music by MAE BOREN AXTON,
TOMMY DURDEN and ELVIS PRESLEY

HELLO MARY LOU

Words and Music by GENE PITNEY
and C. MANGIARACINA

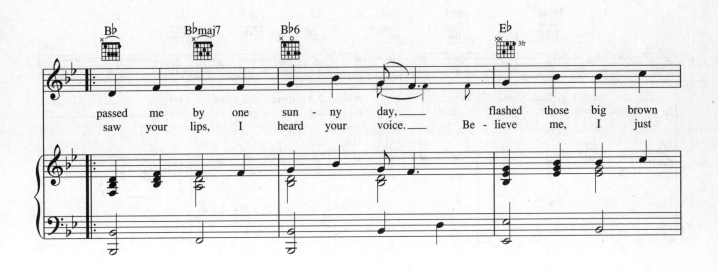

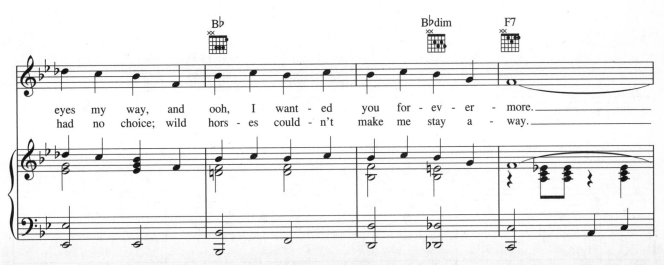

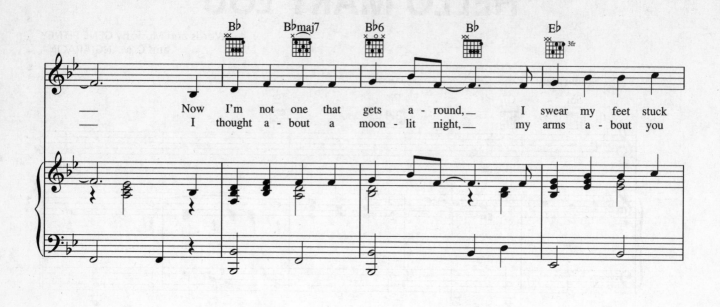

Now I'm not one that gets a - round,___ I swear my feet stuck
I thought a - bout a moon - lit night,___ my arms a - bout you

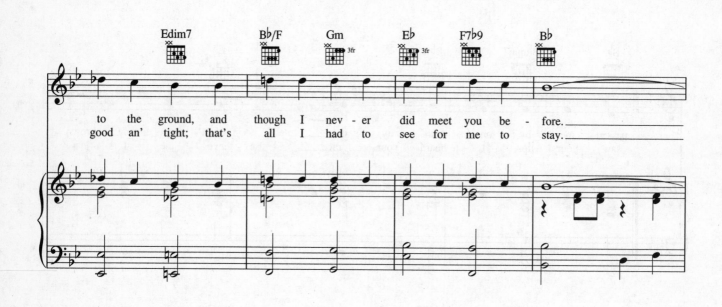

to the ground, and though I nev - er did meet you be - fore.___
good an' tight; that's all I had to see for me to stay.___

I said, "Hel - lo, Ma - ry Lou, good - bye,

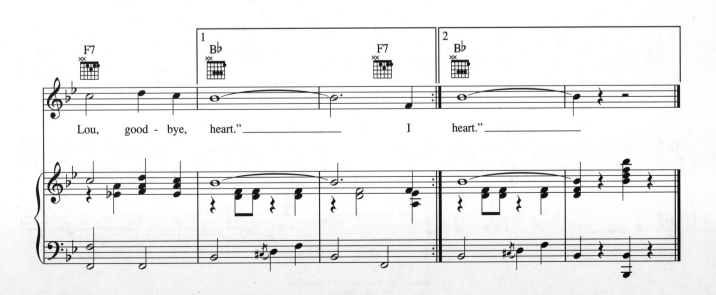

HI-HEEL SNEAKERS

Words and Music by
ROBERT HIGGENBOTHAM

HOUND DOG

Words and Music by JERRY LEIBER
and MIKE STOLLER

Moderate Shuffle

You ain't noth-in' but a hound dog, ___ cry-in' all the

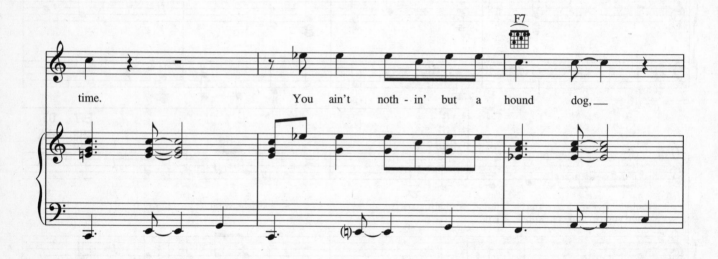

time. You ain't noth-in' but a hound dog, ___

cry-in' all the time. Well ___ you ain't

I GET AROUND

Words and Music by BRIAN WILSON
and MIKE LOVE

same ol' strip,__ I got-ta find a new place where the kids are hip.__
nev-er been beat__ and__ we've nev-er missed yet with the girls we meet.__

My bud-dies and me__ are get-tin'
None of the guys go stead-y 'cause it

real well-known,__ yeah, the bad guys know us and they leave us a-lone.__ } I get a-
would-n't be right__ to leave your best girl home on a Sat-ur-day night.__

C   A7

round_____ from town to town._____

IN MY ROOM

Words and Music by BRIAN WILSON
and GARY USHER

IN THE MIDNIGHT HOUR

Words and Music by STEVE CROPPER
and WILSON PICKETT

IT'S MY PARTY

Words and Music by HERB WIENER,
WALLY GOLD and JOHN GLUCK, JR.

Moderately bright

No - bod - y knows__ where_ my John - ny has gone,__ "But
Play all my rec - ords, keep danc - ing all night,__ But
Ju - dy and John - ny just walked thru the door,__

Ju - dy left__ the same time.
leave me a - lone__ for a while,
Like a queen__ with her king,

Why was he
'Til John - ny's
Oh, what a

JAILHOUSE ROCK

Words and Music by JERRY LEIBER
and MIKE STOLLER

126

Additional Lyrics

2. Spider Murphy played the tenor saxophone
Little Joe was blowin' on the slide trombone.
The drummer boy from Illinois went crash, boon, bang;
The whole rhythm section was the Purple Gang.
(Chorus)

3. Number Forty-seven said to number Three:
"You're the cutest jailbird I ever did see.
I sure would be delighted with your company,
Come on and do the Jailhouse Rock with me."
(Chorus)

4. The sad sack was a-sittin' on a block of stone,
Way over in the corner weeping all alone.
The warden said: "Hey, Buddy, don't you be no square,
If you can't find a partner, use a wooden chair!"
(Chorus)

5. Shifty Henry said to Bugs: "For heaven's sake,
No one's lookin', now's our chance to make a break."
Bugsy turned to Shifty and he said: "Nix, nix;
I wanna stick around a while and get my kicks."
(Chorus)

KANSAS CITY

Words and Music by JERRY LEIBER
and MIKE STOLLER

LA BAMBA

By RITCHIE VALENS

LIMBO ROCK

Words and Music by BILLY STRANGE
and JON SHELDON

lim - bo boy __ and girl   all a - round the lim - bo world   gon - na
spread your lim - bo feet,   then you move to lim - bo beat.   Lim - bo
self a lim - bo girl,   give that chick a lim - bo whirl.   There's a

LAST KISS

Words and Music by
WAYNE COCHRAN

LITTLE DEUCE COUPE

Music by BRIAN WILSON
Words by ROGER CHRISTIAN

THE LOCO-MOTION

Words and Music by GERRY GOFFIN
and CAROLE KING

Moderately fast

Ev-'ry-bod-y's do - ing a brand - new dance now.

(Come on, ba - by, do the Lo - co - mo - tion.) I

know you'll get to like it if you give it a chance now.

THE LOCO-MOTION

(Come on, ba - by, do _____ the Lo - co - mo - tion.) My

Guitar → F
(capo 3rd
fret)
Piano → Ab

Dm
Fm

F
Ab

lit - tle ba - by sis - ter can do it with ease. _ It's eas - i - er than learn - ing your

D
F

C
Eb

G
Bb

A - B - C's. _ So come on, come on, and do _____ the Lo - co - mo - tion with me. _

C
Eb

F
Ab

You've got to swing your hips now. _ (Come on.) Come on.
Instrumental...

LONG TALL SALLY

Words and Music by ENOTRIS JOHNSON,
RICHARD PENNIMAN and ROBERT BLACKWELL

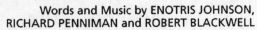

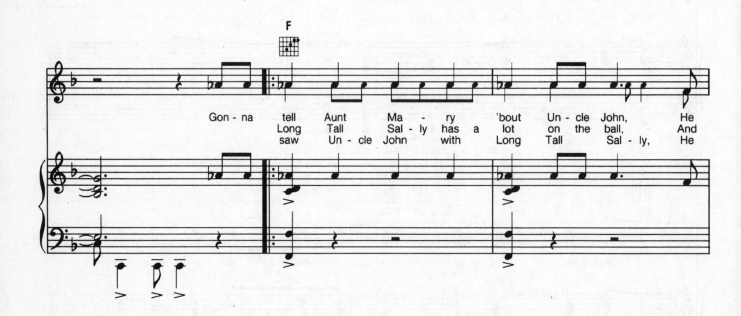

Gon-na tell Aunt Ma-ry 'bout Un-cle John, He
Long Tall Sal-ly has a lot on the ball, And
saw Un-cle John with Long Tall Sal-ly, He

says he has the blues, But he has a lot of fun, Oh,
no-bod-y cares if she's long and tall, Oh,
saw Aunt Ma-ry com-in' And he ducked back in the al-ley, Oh,

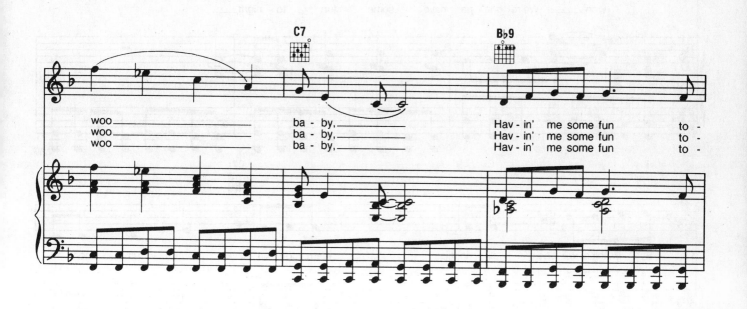

OH, LONESOME ME

Words and Music by
DON GIBSON

LOUIE, LOUIE

Words and Music by
RICHARD BERRY

MATCHBOX

Words and Music by
CARL LEE PERKINS

MY BOYFRIEND'S BACK

Words and Music by ROBERT FELDMAN,
GERALD GOLDSTEIN and RICHARD GOTTEHRER

NO PARTICULAR PLACE TO GO

Words and Music by
CHUCK BERRY

wild.
ear.
stroll.
budge.

Cruis - ing and play - ing the ra - di - o,
Cud - dling more and driv - ing slow,
Can you im - ag - ine the way I felt?
Cruis - ing and play - ing the ra - di - o,

with no par - tic - u - lar place to go.
with no par - tic - u - lar place to go.
I couldn't un - fas - ten her safe - ty belt.
with no par - tic - u - lar place to

Rid - ing a - long in my au - to - mo - go.
No par - tic - u - lar place to
Rid - ing a - long in my cal - a -

PEGGY SUE

Words and Music by JERRY ALLISON,
NORMAN PETTY and BUDDY HOLLY

Oh, well, I love you, gal,___ Yes, I love you, Peg - gy Sue:___

Peg - gy Sue,___

Peg - gy Sue,___ Pret - ty, pret - ty, pret - ty, pret - ty,

Peg - gy Sue,___ Oh, my Peg - gy,___ My

177

(You've Got)
PERSONALITY

Words and Music by LLOYD PRICE
and HAROLD LOGAN

RETURN TO SENDER

Words and Music by OTIS BLACKWELL
and WINFIELD SCOTT

Moderate Rhythm and Blues

I gave a let-ter to the post - man; _____ he put it in his
So then I dropped it in the mail - box _____ and sent it Spe - cial

sack.
D.
Bright and ear - ly next morn - ing _____ he
Bright and ear - ly next morn - ing _____ it

brought my let - ter back.
came right back to me.
She wrote up - on it: Re - turn _____ to send - er

PLEASE MR. POSTMAN

Words and Music by ROBERT BATEMAN,
GEORGIA DOBBINS, WILLIAM GARRETT,
FREDDIE GORMAN and BRIAN HOLLAND

188

THE PROMISED LAND

Words and Music by
CHUCK BERRY

2nd Verse

Right away I Bought me A through train ticket,
Ridin' across Mississippi clean,
And I was on the Midnight Flyer out of Birmingham,
Smokin' into New Orleans.
Somebody helped me get out of Louisiana,
Just to help me get to Houston Town.
There are people there who care a little about me,
And they won't let a poor boy down,
Sure as you're born, they bought me a silk suit,
They put luggage in my hand,
And I woke up high over Albuquerque on a jet
   to the Promised Land.

3rd Verse

Workin' on a T. bone steak,
I had a party flyin' over to the Golden State,
When the pilot told us in thirteen minutes
He would get us at the Terminal Gate.
Swing low, chariot, come down easy,
Taxi to the Terminal Line;
Cut your engines, and cool your wings,
And let me make it to the telephone,
Los Angeles, give me Norfolk, Virginia,
Tidewater 4-10-0-0,
Tell the folks back home this is the Promised Land
   callin' and the poor boy's on the line.

ROCK AND ROLL IS HERE TO STAY

Words and Music by
DAVID WHITE

Rock, Rock, Rock, oh, ba-by,

Rock, Rock, Rock, oh, ba-by, Rock, Rock,

Rock, oh, ba-by, Rock, Rock, Rock, oh, ba-by.

peo - ple say, ___ rock and roll is here to stay. ___
al - ways be, ___ it' - ll go down in his - to - ry. ___
have a ball, ___ ev - 'ry - bod - y rock and roll. ___

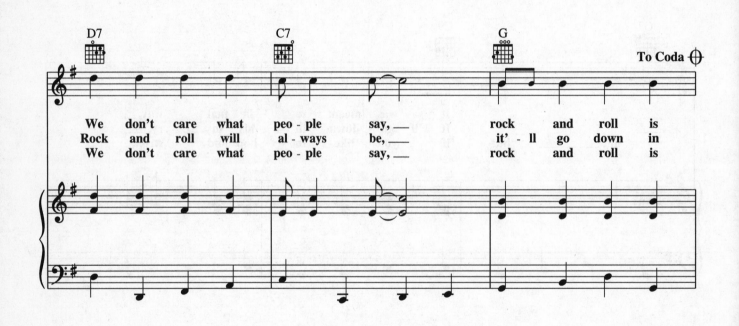

We don't care what peo - ple say, ___ rock and roll is
Rock and roll will al - ways be, ___ it' - ll go down in
We don't care what peo - ple say, ___ rock and roll is

To Coda ⊕

1.
here to stay. ___

2.
his - to - ry. ___ Ev - 'ry - bod - y

A ROSE AND A BABY RUTH

Words and Music by
JOHN D. LOUDERMILK

Moderately slow

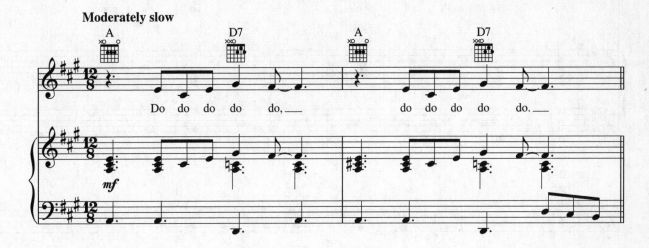

Do do do do do, ___ do do do do do. ___

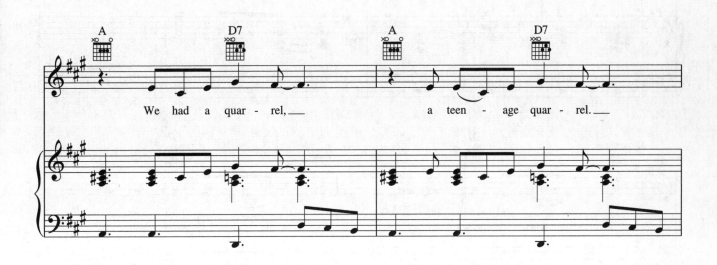

We had a quar-rel, ___ a teen-age quar-rel. ___

Now I'm as blue ___ as I know how ___ to be.

ROCK AROUND THE CLOCK

Words and Music by MAX C. FREEDMAN
and JIMMY DeKNIGHT

RUNAWAY

Words and Music by DEL SHANNON
and MAX CROOK

SEA OF LOVE

Words and Music by GEORGE KHOURY
and PHILIP BAPTISTE

Medium Slow Fifties Rock

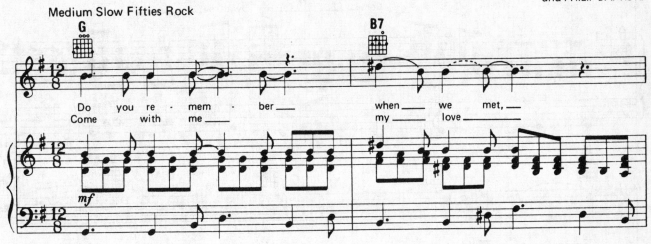

Do you re-mem-ber ___ when ___ we met, ___
Come with me ___ my ___ love ___

that's the day ___ I knew you were my pet.
to the sea, ___ the sea ___ of love. ___

I ___ want to tell you

(just) how ___ much ___ I love you ___

To Coda

207

SAVE THE LAST DANCE FOR ME

Words and Music by DOC POMUS
and MORT SHUMAN

SEARCHIN'

Words and Music by JERRY LEIBER
and MIKE STOLLER

SHAKE, RATTLE AND ROLL

Words and Music by
CHARLES CALHOUN

SINCERELY

Words and Music by ALAN FREED
and HARVEY FUQUA

SHOUT

Words and Music by O'KELLY ISLEY,
RONALD ISLEY and RUDOLPH ISLEY

228

234

SILHOUETTES

Words and Music by FRANK C. SLAY JR.
and BOB CREWE

SINGING THE BLUES

Words and Music by
MELVIN ENDSLEY

SPLISH SPLASH

Moderately, with a beat

Words and Music by BOBBY DARIN
and MURRAY KAUFMAN

Splish splash, I was
Bing bang, ___ I

tak - in' a bath ___
saw the whole gang ___

'Long a - bout - a Sat - ur - day
Danc - in' on my liv - in' room

night.
rug. (Yeah)

A rub dub, just re - lax - in' in the tub,
Flip flop, they were do - in' the bop,

All the

how was I to know there was a par - ty go - ing on?
went and put my danc - ing shoes___

on I was a - splish - in' and a - splash - in', I was a -

roll - in' and a - stroll - in', I was a - mov - in' and a - groov - in',

Repeat and Fade

I was a - reel - in' with the feel - in' I was a -

SIXTEEN CANDLES

Words and Music by LUTHER DIXON
and ALLYSON R. KHENT

SLEEPWALK

By SANTO FARINA,
JOHN FARINA and ANN FARINA

SLIPPIN' AND SLIDIN'

Words and Music by RICHARD PENNIMAN, EDWIN BOCAGE,
ALBERT COLLINS and JAMES SMITH

Slip-pin' and a-slid-in', peep-in' and a-hid-in', been told a long time a-
Oh, __ big con-niv-er, noth-in' but a jiv-er, done got __ hip to your
Oh, __ Ma-lin-da, she's a sol-id send-er, you know you bet-ter sur-
Slip-pin' and a-slid-in', peep-in' and a-hid-in', been told a long time a-

SPOOKY

Words and Music by J.R. COBB, BUDDY BUIE,
HARRY MIDDLEBROOKS and MIKE SHAPIRO

You al-ways keep me guess-ing, I nev - er seem to know what you are

think - ing, And if a fel - ler looks at you, it's for

sure your lit - tle eye will be a - wink-ing.

I get con - fused____'cause I don't know where I stand____ and then you

STAGGER LEE

Words and Music by LLOYD PRICE
and HAROLD LOGAN

The night was clear and the moon was yel-low,___ and the leaves came tum-bling down.

I was stand-ing___ on the cor-ner___ when I
Lee___ told Bil - ly,___ "I can't
Lee___ went to the bar-room,___ and he

heard my bull-dog bark. He was bark-ing at the two men who were
let you go with that. You have won all my___ mon-ey and my
stood a-cross the bar-room door. Said, "Now no-bod-y move,"___ and he

STAND BY ME

Words and Music by BEN E. KING,
JERRY LEIBER and MIKE STOLLER

SURFIN' U.S.A.

Words and Music by
CHUCK BERRY

STAY

Words and Music by
MAURICE WILLIAMS

STUPID CUPID

Words and Music by HOWARD GREENFIELD
and NEIL SEDAKA

TAKE GOOD CARE OF MY BABY

Words and Music by GERRY GOFFIN
and CAROLE KING

TEARS ON MY PILLOW

Words and Music by SYLVESTER BRADFORD
and AL LEWIS

Moderate 12/8 feel

You don't re-mem-ber me ___ but I re-mem-ber you ___

'Twas not so long a-go ___ you broke my heart in two ___

Tears ___ on my pil-low ___ pain ___ in my heart ___ Caused by

TEEN ANGEL

Words and Music by
JEAN SURREY

A TEENAGER IN LOVE

Words and Music by DOC POMUS
and MORT SHUMAN

TEQUILA

By CHUCK RIO

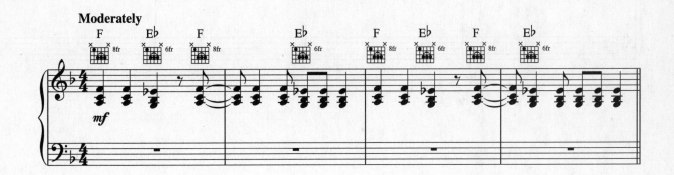

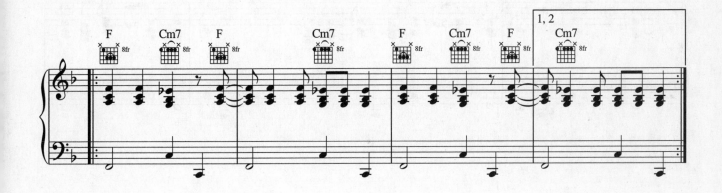

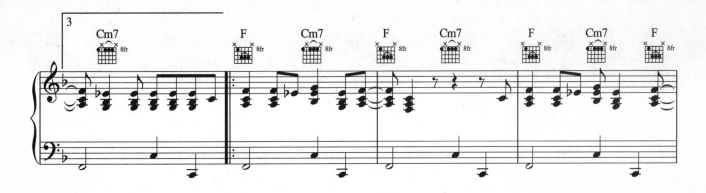

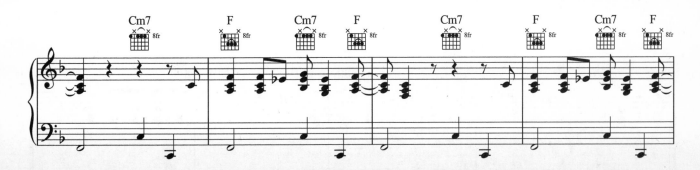

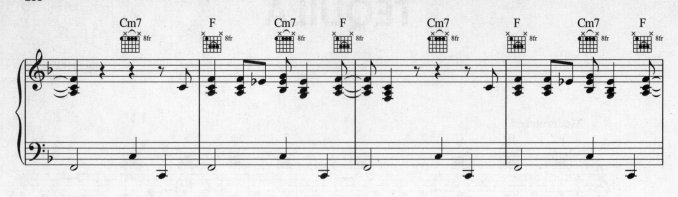

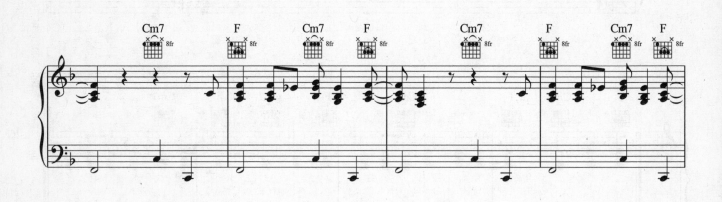

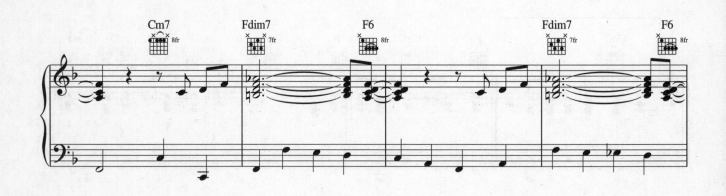

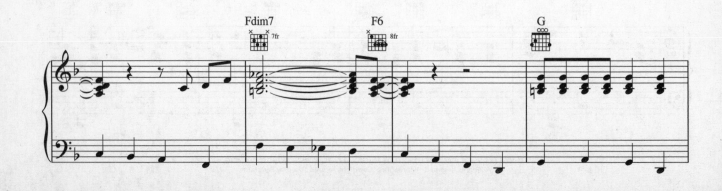

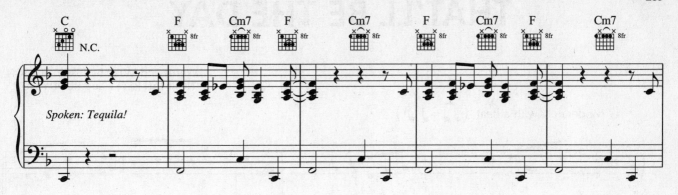

Spoken: *Tequila!*

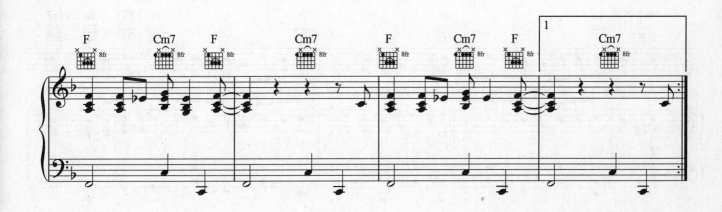

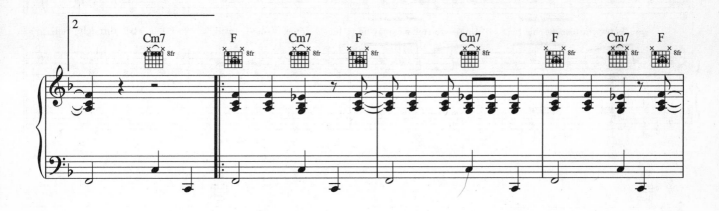

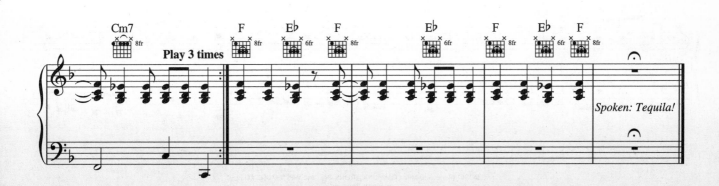

Play 3 times

Spoken: *Tequila!*

THAT'LL BE THE DAY

Words and Music by JERRY ALLISON,
NORMAN PETTY and BUDDY HOLLY

Moderately with a Beat

Well, you give me all your lov-in' and your tur-tle-dov-in', All__ your hugs an' kiss-es an' your mon-ey too; Well,

you know you love me, ba - by, Un-til you tell me, may-be, that some day, well, I'll be through! Well,__

That - 'll Be The Day, when you say, good - bye, Yes,____ That - 'll Be The Day, when

TRAVELIN' MAN

Words and Music by
JERRY FULLER

turn. Pret-ty Pol-y-ne-sian ba-by o-ver the sea, ___

I re-mem-ber the night ___ when we walked on the sands of

Wai-ki-ki ___ and I held you, oh, so tight. ___ I'm a

N.C.

Optional Ending
E♭

Repeat ad lib. and Fade

{ Oh, ___ } I'm a trav-el-in' man. _
{ Yes, ___ }

UNDER THE BOARDWALK

Words and Music by ARTIE RESNICK
and KENNY YOUNG

TUTTI FRUTTI

Words and Music by LITTLE RICHARD PENNIMAN
and DOROTHY LA BOSTRIE

THE TWIST

Words and Music by
HANK BALLARD

Moderately fast '50s Rock

TWIST AND SHOUT

Words and Music by BERT RUSSELL
and PHIL MEDLEY

Moderately, with a beat

Well, shake it up ba - by, __ now,)
- by, __ now, }(Shake it up ba - by) Twist and
ba - by, __ now,

shout. __ (Twist and shout) __ Come on, come on, __ come on, __ come on,

WHY DO FOOLS FALL IN LOVE

Words and Music by MORRIS LEVY
and FRANKIE LYMON

WILD THING

Words and Music by
CHIP TAYLOR

WILD THING,

You make my heart sing.

You make eve - ry - thing __ groov - y. __

Repeat and Fade

WILD THING.

YAKETY YAK

Words and Music by JERRY LEIBER
and MIKE STOLLER

* When no vocal

YOUNG LOVE

Words and Music by
RIC CARTEY

WILLIE AND THE HAND JIVE

Words and Music by
JOHNNY OTIS